INTRODUCTION TO PAINTING

A STEP BY STEP GUIDE

BY JOHN HENN

CHARTWELL
BOOKS, INC.

A QUINTET BOOK

ISBN: 0-7858-0330-0

This book was designed and produced by
Quintet Publishing Limited
6, Blundell Street
London N7 9BH

Jacket Design: Nik Morley

Typeset in Great Britain by
Central Southern Typesetters, Eastbourne
Manufactured in China by
Regent Publishing Services Ltd.

This edition produced for sale in the USA,
its territories and dependencies only.

Published by Chartwell Books
A Division of Book Sales, Inc.
P.O. Box 7100
Edison, New Jersey 08818–7100

Contents

Payne's grey and cadmium yellow.

Prussian blue and cadmium yellow.

Cobalt and cadmium yellow.

Prussian blue and lemon yellow.

Viridian and lemon.

Black and cadmium yellow.

Cobalt blue and alizarin crimson.

Payne's grey and alizarin crimson.

Prussian blue and alizarin crimson.

Cobalt blue and Payne's grey.

Black and Prussian blue.

Black and alizarin crimson.

Cadmium yellow and cadmium red.

Alizarin crimson and cadmium yellow.

Lemon yellow and cadmium red.

Burnt umber and black.

Payne's grey and cadmium red.

Burnt umber and cobalt blue.

WATERCOLOUR EQUIPMENT

PERHAPS THE GREATEST single advantage of watercolour painting is that only a small amount of equipment is needed, equipment which is easy to store. Paints and brushes, although not cheap, last for a long time; indeed brushes should last virtually for ever if looked after.

♦ PAINTS AND COLOURS ♦

Ready-made watercolour paint is sold in various forms, the commonest being tubes, pans and half-pans. These all contain glycerine and are known as semi-moist colours, unlike the traditional dry cakes, which are still available in some artist's suppliers, but are not much used today. Dry cakes require considerable rubbing with water before the colour is released. It is a slow process, but the paints are therefore economical.

Gouache paints, or designer's colours as they are sometimes called, are normally sold in tubes. These paints, and the cheaper versions of them, poster colours and powder paints, have chalk added to the pigment to thicken it, and are thus opaque, unlike true watercolour. Water-colours themselves can be mixed with Chinese white to make them opaque or semi-opaque, so that they become a softer and more subtle form of gouache.

Success in watercolour painting depends so much on applying layers of transparent, but rich, colour that it is a mistake to buy any but the best-quality paints, known as 'artist's quality'. There are cheaper paints, sold for 'sketching', but since these contain a filler to extend the pigment, the colour is weaker and the paint tends to be chalky and unpredictable in use.

Whether to use pans, half-pans or tubes is a personal choice. Each type has its advantages and disadvantages. Tubes are excellent for those who work mainly indoors on a fairly large scale, as any quantity of paint can be squeezed out of them on to the palette. Any paint left on the palette after a painting is completed can be used again later, simply by moistening it with a wet brush. Pans and half-pans, which can be bought in sets in their own palette and are easy to carry, are the most popular choice for working out of doors on a small scale. Watercolours can also be bought in concentrated form in bottles, with droppers to transfer the paint to the palette. These are eminently suitable for broad washes which require a large quantity of paint, but they are less easy to mix than the other types.

The choice of colours is also personal, though there are some colours that everyone must have. Nowadays there is such a vast range of colours to choose from that a beginner is justified in feeling somewhat bewildered, but, in fact, only a few are really necessary. One point to bear in mind is that some colours are considerably less permanent than

ABOVE A pocket set of watercolours is particularly useful when painting out of doors, or when travelling.

LEFT: These swatches show some of the effects that can be achieved by mixing in a limited colour range.

ABOVE Semi-moist pans must be carried in tins and boxes, which can then be used as palettes.

BELOW MIDDLE Half pans are available individually as well as in sets. The artist can replace the most frequently used colours, and also build up a palette to suit his own style.

ABOVE Bottled watercolours are concentrated, and quicker to use than dry cakes or semi-moist pans when a large area of wash is required.

RIGHT Watercolour in tube form is popular and convenient. Do not squeeze too many colours onto your palette at a time, or they will run together.

LEFT Gouache is available in tube or pot form in an enormous range of colours. From left to right: lamp black, zinc white, burnt sienna, raw umber, yellow ochre, cadmium red (pale) cadmium yellow (pale), Winsor emerald, cobalt blue.

others, which may not be an important consideration for quick sketches and 'note-taking', but clearly is for any painting that is intended to be hung or exhibited. A wise course, therefore, is to rule out any colours classified as 'fugitive'. All the major paint manufacturers have systems of grading permanence. These are not always marked on the tubes or pans, but they appear on the manufacturers' colour charts; if in doubt, ask the shopkeeper or manager for advice. The tubes or pans will also bear a code indicating the relative price of each colour, some being more expensive than others according to the cost of the pigment used.

The golden rule when choosing a range of colours, or 'palette' as professionals call it, is to keep it as simple as possible. Few watercolourists use more than a dozen colours. For landscape painting, useful additions to the basic palette are sap green, Hooker's green, raw umber and cerulean blue, while monastral blue (called Winsor blue in the Winsor and Newton range) is sometimes recommended instead of Prussian blue. For flower painting the basic range might be enlarged by the addition of cobalt violet and lemon yellow.

◆ PAPER ◆

The traditional support — the term used for the surface on which any painting is done — is white or pale-coloured paper, which reflects back through the transparent paint to give the translucent quality so characteristic of watercolours. There are many types of watercolour paper. Each individual will probably need to try several before establishing which one suits his method of working, though sometimes a particular paper may be chosen to create a special effect.

The three main types of machine-made paper are hot-pressed (HP), cold-pressed (CP), which is also rather quaintly known as 'not' for 'not hot-pressed' and rough. Hot-pressed paper is very smooth and, although suitable

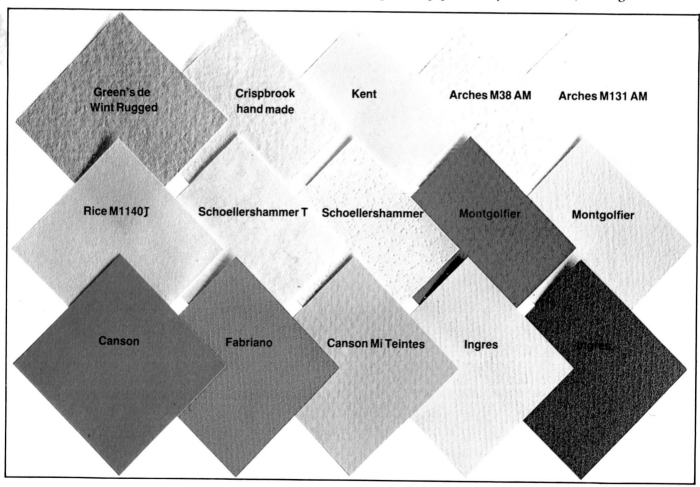

Green's de Wint Rugged

Crispbrook hand made

Kent

Arches M38 AM

Arches M131 AM

Rice M1140J

Schoellershammer T

Schoellershammer

Montgolfier

Montgolfier

Canson

Fabriano

Canson Mi Teintes

Ingres

Ingres

ABOVE The range of papers available is vast and can be bewildering even for the experienced artist. In order to find the paper which suits your particular style and immediate needs, buy only a few sheets at a time. The heavier papers are more expensive but can absorb large amounts of water; they do not, therefore, need stretching, which makes them useful for outdoor work. Toned papers provide a convenient middle ground for some subjects, from which to work darks and lights.

for drawing or pen-and-wash, is not a good choice for building up layers of washes in the standard watercolour technique as it becomes clogged very quickly. Cold-pressed paper, which is slightly textured, is the most popular and is suitable for both broad washes and fine detail. Rough paper, as its name implies, is much more heavily textured, and the paint will settle in the 'troughs' while sliding off the 'peaks', giving a speckled effect which can be effective for some subjects but is difficult to exploit successfully. Among the best-known makes of good water-colour papers are Saunders, Fabriano, Arches, Bockingford, Strathmore in the US, Ingres in the UK, and R.W.S. (Royal Watercolour Society), some of which also include hand-made papers.

Hand-made papers are made from pure linen rag and specially treated with size to provide the best possible surface for watercolour work. Such papers are sized on one side only and thus have a right and a wrong side, which can be checked by holding the paper up to the light so that the watermark becomes visible. Many of the better machine-made papers also have a watermark and hence a right and wrong side.

Some papers have surfaces which are tough enough to withstand a great deal of preliminary drawing and rubbing out without damage, but others do not. Bockingford paper, for instance, although excellent in many ways, is quickly damaged by erasing, and the paint will take on a patchy appearance wherever the surface has been spoiled. One of its advantages, however, is that paint can easily be removed by washing out where necessary; the paint, moreover, can be manipulated and moved around in a very free way. Arches paper and Saunders paper are both strong enough to stand up to erasing, but mistakes are difficult to remove from the former, which holds the paint very firmly. Saunders paper is a good choice for beginners: it is strong, stretches well and has a pleasant surface with enough grain to give a little, but not too much, texture.

◆ STRETCHING THE PAPER ◆

Watercolour papers vary widely in weight, or thickness, and the lighter ones need to be stretched or they will buckle as soon as wet paint is applied to them. The weight is usually expressed in pounds and refers to the weight of a ream (480 sheets), not to each individual sheet. The thinner papers, ranging from 70 to 140 pounds, must be stretched; any paper weighing 200 pounds or more can be used without this treatment. Watercolour boards can be bought. These have watercolour paper mounted on heavy board, so that the stretching has already been done. They are particularly useful for outdoor work, since no drawing board is needed.

Stretching paper is not difficult, but since the paper must be soaked, it takes some time to dry thoroughly and needs to be done at least two hours before you intend to start work. Cut the paper to the size required (if you do not want to use the whole sheet) and wet it well on both sides by laying it in a bath or tray of water. When it is well soaked, hold it up by the corners to drain off the excess

STRETCHING PAPER.

1. *Cut the paper to size and place it right-side up in a bath or tray of water. Leave it to soak for a few minutes.*

2. *Lift out the paper and drain off the excess water.*

3. *Lay the paper on a drawing board at least 1 in/2.5 cm larger than the paper all around. Make sure that the paper is still the right way up.*

4. *Smooth the paper quite flat and stick gumstrip around the edges, starting with opposite sides.*

5. *Finish by putting a drawing pin in each corner. Do not dry the paper in front of a fire, which will buckle it.*

water, then lay it right-side-up on a drawing board and stick down each edge with the gummed brown paper known as gumstrip (do not use masking tape or sellotape). Finally, place a drawing pin in each corner. The paper will dry taut and flat and should not buckle when paint is applied. Occasionally, however, stretching does go wrong and the paper buckles at one corner or tears away from the gumstrip; if that happens there is no other course but to repeat the process. Drying can be hastened with a hair-drier, but it is not a good practice to leave the board in front of a fire. Ideally the paper should dry naturally.

The differences between a quality sable brush (left), or synthetic sable (middle), and the kind of cheap brush sometimes provided in watercolour boxes (right), are self-evident.

◆ BRUSHES ◆

Soft brushes are normally used for watercolour. The best ones are sable, made from the tips of the tail hairs of the small rodent found chiefly in Siberia. Sable brushes are extremely expensive, but if looked after properly they should last a lifetime. Watercolour brushes are also made from squirrel-hair (known as 'camel hair' for some reason) and ox-hair. These are good substitutes for sable, but have less spring. There is now a wide range of synthetic brushes, usually made of nylon or a mixture of nylon and sable, and although they do not hold the paint as well as sable and are thus less suitable for broad washes, they are excellent for finer details and are very much chaper.

Brushes come in a variety of shapes and only by experiment will an individual discover which shapes and sizes suit him. It is not necessary to have a great many brushes for watercolour work; for most purposes three or four will be adequate, and many artists use only two. A practical range would be one large chisel-end for laying washes and two or three rounds in different sizes. Some watercolourists use ordinary household brushes for washes, but care must be taken to prevent hairs from falling out as you work.

If you want your brushes to last, it is essential to look

BELOW Soft sable brushes are the best brushes, but they are very expensive and many synthetic and sable and synthetic mixtures are now available. A beginner should not need more than one flat brush and two or three rounds; specialized brushes such as blenders and fans are used for particular techniques.

Japanese and Chinese brushes are versatile, and are very well suited to fine calligraphic work, but they require some practice and are not recommended for beginners.

LEFT *The complete range of sizes available of one make of brush.*

BELOW *A range of brush types used for particular techniques. From left to right: fine synthetic round, broad synthetic round, mixed fibres round, ox hair round, squirrel hair round, sable fan, sable bright, sable round, fine sable round.*

after them well. Wash them thoroughly in running water after use — if they are still stained use a little soap. Never leave brushes pointing downwards in a glass of water, as this will bend the hairs out of shape, possibly permanently. If they need to be stored for a length of time in a box or tin make sure that they are absolutely dry; otherwise mildew may form. Store them upright if possible.

ABOVE A suggested 'starter palette'. From right to left: white (above), yellow ochre, cadmium yellow, cadmium red, alizarin crimson, cobalt violet, ultramarine, Prussian blue and viridian.

The palette chosen depends very much on the subject to be painted: for instance, violet might not be needed at all, cobalt blue might be used instead of the other two blues, an additional green, such as chrome oxide, added, and a different yellow chosen.

The photograph shows the colours mixed with varying amounts of white.

OIL PAINTING EQUIPMENT

M ATERIALS for oil painting can be costly; so it is advisable to work out your 'starter kit' carefully. Begin by buying the minimum and adding extra colours, brushes and so on when you have progressed to the stage of understanding your particular requirements. For example, someone who intends to specialize in flower painting will need a different range of colours from someone whose chosen theme is seascapes, while a person working on a miniature scale will use brushes quite unlike those needed for large-scale paintings.

CHOOSING PAINTS

Oil paints are divided into two main categories: artists' and students' colours. The latter are cheaper because they contain less pure pigment and more fillers and extenders, but in general they are a false economy for that very reason; they cannot provide the same intensity of colour as the more expensive range. However, students' colours are fine for practising with, and it is possible to combine the two types using the students' colours for browns and other colours where intensity is not a prime requirement and artists' for the pure colours such as red, yellow and blue. A large-size tube of white works out most economical, since white is used more than most other colours.

Paints in the artists' range are not all the same price – a trap for the unwary. They are classified in series, usually from 1 to 7 (different manufacturers have different methods of classification), series 7 being extremely expensive. The price differences reflect the expense and/or scarcity of the pigment used.

It is often said that all colours can be mixed from the three primaries, red, yellow and blue. To some extent this is true, but they will certainly not provide a subtle or exciting range, and in any case there are a great many different versions of red, yellow and blue. The illustration shows a suggested 'starter palette', which should provide an adequate mix of colours for most purposes. In general you will need, as well as white, a warm and a cool version of each of the primaries, plus a brown and a green and perhaps a violet or purple. Strictly speaking, greens are not essential as they can be mixed from blue and yellow, but it takes time and experience to arrive at the right hue, and there really is not much point in spending more time in mixing than you need. Vividian is a good choice, since it mixes well with any colour. Other useful additions to your palette are rose madder in the red group; a lemon yellow such as Winsor or cadmium lemon in the yellow group; cerulean blue and Antwerp or cobalt blue in the blue group; and sap green and chrome green in the greens. Good browns and greys are burnt sienna, burnt umber and Payne's grey. Flake white dries quickly and is resistant to cracking, but it contains poisonous lead; for this reason some artists prefer to use titanium white, which is non-toxic. The use of black is often frowned upon, and many artists never use it as it can have a deadening effect, but it can be mixed with yellow to produce a rich olive green, and many landscape artists use it for this purpose.

PAINTING MEDIUMS

Oil paint can be used just as it comes from the tube, or it can be a combination of oil and a thinner (what artists call a *medium*). If you try to apply undiluted paint accurately in a small area, you will see why such mediums are necessary; without them the paint is not easily malleable.

The most popular medium is the traditional blend of linseed oil and turpentine or white spirit, usually in a ratio of 60% oil and 40% thinner. Linseed oil dries to a glossy finish which is resistant to cracking – but be sure to buy either purified or cold-pressed linseed oil, which dry without yellowing. Boiled linseed oil – the sort found in DIY shops – contains impurities which cause rapid yellowing.

Linseed oil is slow to dry, which may not suit your way of working and can produce a rather churned-up paint surface. There are several faster-drying mediums available, such as drying linseed oil, drying poppy oil, stand oil (which also makes the paint flow well and disguises brushstrokes) and an alkyd-based medium sold under the name of *Liquin*.

Turpentine is the most commonly used artist's thinner, though in fact white spirit is just as good and is less likely to cause the headaches and allergic reactions which artists sometimes complain of when using turpentine. White spirit also has less odour, and stores without deteriorating.

Special ready-mixed painting mediums are sold for specific purposes. Linseed oil, for instance, is not suitable for glazing as it will dribble down the surface of the canvas, but Liquin is excellent for this purpose. Another alkyd medium, *Oleopasto,* has been developed specially for impasto work. It is designed to extend the paint and add body to it so that it can be applied in thick layers, with the brush or knife marks clearly visible.

BRUSHES AND KNIVES

Paint brushes for oil painting come in a wide range of shapes, sizes and materials. Good-quality brushes cost more, but are worth the initial outlay as they last longer and hold their shape better. For oils, unlike for watercolours, you need more than just one or two brushes, otherwise you will be forever cleaning them between applying one colour and the next. The ideal is to have one brush for each colour, but a selection of six should be enough to start off with.

RIGHT A selection of palette and painting knives. Second from the left is the standard palette knife, which is designed mainly for cleaning the palette and mixing paint, but can also be used for applying paint to the support. The others are all specifically designed for painting. As with brushes, some experimentation is needed to find out which shape suits which individual; some artists never use painting knives at all.

PAINTBOXES

Theoretically, any old cardboard box will do to keep paints, brushes and media in, but if you are intending to carry paints around with you it is worth investing in a proper box with separate compartments for paints and brushes. Most of these are wooden, with a carrying handle, and are sold with their own palette which fits into the lid.

Alternatively you can improvize your own paintbox from a toolbox or fishing tackle box, which are less expensive and lighter to carry.

OIL PAINTING ACCESSORIES

Other essential items include dippers for your painting medium, which can be attached to the palette; jam jars or tin cans to hold white spirit for cleaning brushes; and of course a large supply of rags or kitchen paper (oil paint is very messy and needs to be cleaned up frequently).

Another useful painting aid is a mahl stick, which steadies your hand when you are painting small details or fine lines. The traditional mahl stick has a bamboo handle with a chamois cushion at one end. The stick is held across the canvas with the cushioned end resting lightly on a dry area of the painting, and you rest your painting arm on the stick to steady yourself as you paint. Mahl sticks are sold at artists' suppliers, but a piece of dowelling or garden cane with a bundle of rags tied to one end is quite adequate, and can be rested on the side of the canvas or board if the paint surface is wet. Page 65 shows a mahl stick being used.

For anyone who intends to do a lot of outdoor work, a pair of canvas separators is very useful. These are designed to keep two wet canvases apart without damaging the paint, and have a handle for carrying. It is necessary to have two canvases of the same size with you, even if you intend to use only one.

VARNISHES

Ideally, paintings should be varnished to protect them from dust and to restore the colours, which tend to become toned down as the paint dries. Many people associate varnish with that dark-brown, sticky look that was such a feature of Victorian paintings, but several clear synthetic varnishes are now available, both matt and gloss. Most varnishes, however, cannot be applied for at least six months, even a year if the paint is very thick, as it takes this long for it to dry out thoroughly. The exceptions are the temporary varnishes, such as retouching varnish, which can be applied when the paint is 'skin dry', that is, in about two weeks to a month. It can also be used to brush over an area that may have become dull and matt during the painting, as sometimes happens, and can be removed if necessary by rubbing gently with distilled turpentine.

BASIC RULES

*E*VERY PAINTER, working in whatever medium, needs to understand the basic rules of his craft, even if sometimes only to break them. The underlying principles of such things as composition, perspective, drawing itself, apply to all kinds of painting. The novice watercolourist, who needs to plan his paintings especially carefully, should have a firm grasp of them from the beginning.

♦ COMPOSING AND SELECTING ♦

Whether you are painting outdoors or indoors, whether your chosen subject is a landscape, a group of buildings, a portrait or a single flower in a vase, you need to have a clear idea of what the main elements are and of how you will place them on the paper before you begin to paint. Painting a landscape out of doors requires you to decide where the view is to begin and end, where to place the horizon, whether to emphasize or alter features in the foreground, and so on. For a portrait, still-life or flower painting you must decide how much to show, the proportion of the figure or flower in relation to the background, the general colour scheme and the balance of lights and darks.

There are well-tested mathematical rules for 'good composition'. The ancient Greeks, for instance, devised the system known as the Golden Section (or Golden Mean), in which the area of the painting is divided by a line in such a way that the smaller part is to the larger what the larger is to the whole. This ensures that the picture plane is divided in a balanced and symmetrical way, and countless artists have made use of the principle. The triangle is another basis for composition (many paintings

ABOVE *Figure paintings are more difficult to compose than landscapes because the choices are so much wider. A figure can be disposed in an almost infinite number of ways, while a landscape often needs only minor re-arranging. Here the artist has placed his subject in the centre of the picture, with the diagonal of the leg balancing the angle of the head. He has allowed one leg and the legs of the chair to 'bust' the frame at the bottom, thus bringing the figure forward on to the picture plane and avoiding a cramped and awkward appearance.*

LEFT Converging lines in landscapes are often used to lead the viewer's eye to the focal point, in this case the buildings. Unusually, the artist has divided the picture into two nearly equal parts, the land and the sky; but monotony has been avoided by allowing the buildings and trees to break into the skyline and by dividing the foreground by the broken line of white road in the middle distance.

tion is one in which there are no jarring elements; all the parts of the picture balance one another in a pleasing way, and the viewer's eye is led into the picture rather than out of it. Whatever the subject, it is almost never advisable to divide the painting into two equal halves, such as sea and land, or table-top and background in a still-life. The result is at once monotonous and disjointed. The viewer's eye should not be led to one part of the painting to the exclusion of others, but there should usually be a 'focal point'. For example, a group of buildings in a landscape can be used simply as a counterpoint to other elements, such as trees and hills, or they may be what interests you most about the scene, with the trees, hills and foreground used as a 'backdrop'. The buildings need not be large, nor placed directly in the centre of the picture (this is not normally advisable); what matters is that the eye should be consistently led to them as the focal point. Compositional devices often used to lead the eye in this way are the curving lines of a path, stream, ploughed field or fence, along which the viewer's eye must travel. Such lines should never lead out of the picture unless for a deliberately sought effect.

The focal point of a portrait is almost always the face, the eyes in particular for a front or three-quarter view, and care must be taken not to detract from it by placing too much emphasis on other elements, such as the background, or the hands. Hands and clothing are often treated in a sketchy way so that they do not assume too much importance. A figure or face should be placed in a well-considered and deliberate way against the background to create a feeling of harmony and balance. There should not be too much space at the top. Nor, usually, should the subject be placed squarely in the middle of the picture, though a central position can sometimes be effective.

Backgrounds are part of a portrait painting, as are skies in landscapes, even when they are quite plain and muted in colour. If a picture is placed against a stark white background, the white areas will have their own shapes and thus make their contribution to the balance of the painting. Such flat areas are known as 'negative space'. A more decorative background, such as a boldly patterned wallpaper or still-life of a vase of flowers on a table, can be used to complement the main subject, just as the colours in the sky or the direction of clouds do in a landscape.

Many artists use viewing frames to help them work out a satisfactory composition, and some also use polaroid cameras for indoor work, taking several shots of a portrait or still-life until they find a satisfactory arrangement. A viewing frame is simply a piece of cardboard with an oblong hole cut in it (a good size of aperture is $4\frac{1}{2} \times 6$ in /11 $\times$ 15 cm), which is held up at about arm's length to work out the best placing of the subject. It is particularly useful for on-the-spot landscape work, as it is very difficult to assess large landscape subjects without some form of framing device. Making small, quick sketches, often referred to as thumbnail sketches, is another good way to work out a composition. A rough scribble, even a few lines, will often provide a clear idea of how the main shapes should be placed within the picture area.

♦ DRAWING ♦

Drawing is the basis of all painting. Indeed, painting is simply drawing with a brush and colour. Although much of the more detailed drawing in a watercolour is done at the final stages with a fine brush, it is nearly always necessary to make some form of pencil drawing on the paper before beginning to paint. Without this, you will have no idea where to place the first wash or which areas to reserve as paler ones. Obviously there are exceptions to this general rule. A very quick study in which colour is the most important aspect or a broad and impressionistic landscape with little detail may not need a drawing. But, even so, a few lines can provide a helpful guide.

Few people draw with the ease and assurance that produce the confident and flowing lines of really fine drawings. However, a drawing which is to be used only as the guideline for a painting need not be of high quality. What matters is getting the proportions and shapes right. Everybody tends to draw what he knows, or thinks he knows, rather than what he actually sees. The first step in drawing is to take a good long look at the subject and try to get rid of any preconceptions about it. By holding a pencil up at arm's length and closing one eye it is possible to check whether a line which appears vertical or horizontal really is so; and the size of one object in relation to another can be measured in the same way. Once one part of a scene, or figure, has been described accurately all the others can be related to it. But if you begin with a false 'statement', misunderstanding the angle at which a roof top slopes away from you, for example, and then try to relate the other shapes and lines to it, the drawing will go progressively awry. It pays to take time over a preliminary drawing, especially if the subject is complex; otherwise you will become increasingly frustrated when you start to paint.

Never try to draw any subject from too close a viewpoint, which distorts the view. And make sure that you do not have to move your head to see different parts of the subject. Your line of vision should be central. Try to make sure that you are reasonably comfortable (not always possible when working out of doors) and hold the drawing board in such a way that it does not obscure any part of the subject. Check sizes and measurements continually by holding up your pencil and moving your thumb up and down on it, closing one eye to measure distances. Avoid making the drawing too fussy. Too many pencil marks may muddy the paint. An HB or B pencil is the best to use, as softer ones may smudge the paper. The drawing can be erased at any stage during the painting.

In portraiture precise drawing is very important. It is often wise to make a preliminary drawing and then transfer it to the painting surface, thus avoiding too much erasing on the surface itself. Here the artist has worked from a photograph, enlarged to the required size by means of a grid. The drawing line transferred to the support by using a form of carbon paper called iron-oxide paper, which provides a clear outline.

WATERCOLOUR TECHNIQUES

♦ **LAYING A FLAT WASH** ♦

*P*URE WATERCOLOUR, being transparent, must be applied from light to dark. The paper itself is used to create the pure white or light tones which, with opaque paints, would be made by using white alone or mixed with coloured pigment.

Any area required to be white is simply 'reserved', or left unpainted, so that when it is surrounded with darker washes it will shine out with great brilliance. Pale tones are created in the same way, with a light-coloured wash put on first and then surrounded with darker tones. Light reflected off the paper, back through these thin skins of paint known as washes, gives a watercolour painting a spontaneity and sparkle which cannot be achieved with any other medium. Hence watercolour's popularity with artists both past and present.

The two most important facts about watercolour are, first, that it is always to some extent unpredictable, even in the hands of experts, and, second, that because dark is always worked over light, some planning is needed before beginning the painting. It is not always necessary to do a detailed and complicated drawing on the paper, only enough to work out the basic shapes and design; this really should be done however, or you will begin without really knowing which areas are to be left white or pale and how they will fit into the painting as a whole.

The wash is the basis of all watercolour painting, whether it is a broad, sweeping one, covering a large expanse, such as a sky or the background to a portrait, or a much smaller one laid on a particular area. Washes need not be totally flat. They can be gradated in both tone and colour, or broken up and varied. But the technique of laying a flat wash must be mastered, even if you subsequently find that you seldom use it.

The support should be tilted at a slight angle so that the brush strokes flow into one another, but do not run down the paper. For a broad wash a large chisel-end brush is normally used; for a smaller one, or a wash which is to be laid against a complicated edge, a smaller round brush may be more manageable. Laying a wash must be done quickly or hard edges will form between brush strokes. Therefore mix up more paint than you think you will need. Start by damping the paper with clear water (this is not actually essential, but helps the paint to go on evenly). Working in one direction, lay a horizontal line of colour at the top of the area, then another below it, working in the opposite direction, and continue working in alternate directions until the area is covered. Never go back over the wet paint because you feel it is uneven or not dark enough, as this will result in the paint's 'flooding' and leave blobs and patches. A final word of caution: if the doorbell or the

FLAT WASH.
A flat wash in a vivid colour is being laid on dampened paper with a broad, flat-ended brush. It is not strictly necessary to dampen the paper (many artists prefer the slightly 'dragged' look given by working on dry paper) but dampening facilitates an even covering. Tilt the board slightly so that the brush strokes flow into one another, and work backwards and forwards down the paper until the whole area is covered.

SPONGE WASH.

Often a wash needs to be slightly textured or varied in strength, for which purpose a sponge is useful.
1. *The wash is mixed with a brush and tested on a piece of spare paper.*

2. *Enough paint is mixed to cover the area and the sponge is dipped into it. For a lighter covering, some of the paint can be squeezed out.*

3. *A variegated effect is achieved by applying the paint quite thickly with the first stroke, much more thinly with the second.*

4. *The final wash can be worked into with the sponge while it is still wet in order to lighten some areas and produce a soft, shimmering effect.*

VARIEGATED WASH.

1. *The paper is dampened with a sponge and a thin wash of colour is applied, also with a sponge.*

2. *A second colour is then flooded on, using the tip of the sponge so that the two run together.*

3. *A brush is now used to touch in darker areas on the still-wet paint. Very subtle effects can be created by this wet-into-wet technique, but they are always to some extent unpredictable.*

telephone rings while you are in the middle of a wash, ignore it; otherwise you will return to a hard edge which is impossible, or at least very difficult to remove.

Leave the wash to dry before working on adjacent areas of the painting. Not until the wash is completely dry will you be able to establish either how even it is or what its true colour value is (watercolour dries much paler than it appears when wet). The ability to assess the precise tone of a wash comes only with experience, but it can be helpful to lay down one or two patches of flat colour on a spare piece of paper and allow them to dry as a preliminary test. Washes can be laid on top of the first one to strengthen the colour or darken the tone, though too many will turn the painting muddy. Purists claim that more than three layers spoils the quality.

Another method of laying a wash is to use a sponge. This is particularly useful when a slightly variegated or textured wash is required, as the sponge can either be filled with paint for a dense covering or used relatively dry for a paler effect. A sponge can also be used in conjunction with a brush. If, for instance, you rinse it in clean water and squeeze it out you can remove some of the paint laid by a brush while it is still wet, thus lightening selected areas — a good technique for skies or distant hills.

♦ PROBLEM-SOLVING ♦

Although watercolours cannot be altered so drastically or so often as paintings in any of the opaque media, changes are possible. It is a mistake to abandon a picture because a first wash has not gone on quite right.

The first thing to remember is that a wash which looks too dark or too vivid on a sheet of otherwise white paper will dry much lighter and may look quite pale when surrounded by other colours. If the first wash looks wrong, let it dry. If you are still quite sure it is not what you intended, sponge it out with a clean sponge and clear water. This may leave a slight stain on the paper, depending on the paper used and the colour itself (some colours stain the paper, like a dye, while others do not) but when dry it will be too faint to spoil the new wash. When a wash has flooded, sponge it out immediately without waiting for it to dry; flooding cannot be entirely remedied, though it can sometimes create an effect not originally planned.

One of the commonest faults is accidentally to take a wash over the edge of an area to be reserved. There are three ways of dealing with this, depending on the size of the area and the type of edge desired. If the wash is pale and the area to be reserved is a broad and imprecise shape, such as a stone in the foreground of a landscape, you can simply sponge out the excess paint with a small sponge or cotton wool damped in clean water. A soft edge will be left. For a more intricate shape, or one requiring a sharp, clear edge, you may have to scrape the paint away (after it is dry) with a razor blade or scalpel, the former for broad areas, the latter for small ones. Hold the blade flat on the paper so that the corners do not dig in and scrape gently. The same method can be used to lighten an area or to create texture by removing a top layer of paint. The third rescue technique — to apply Chinese white with a fine brush — should be used only when the painting is otherwise complete; if the white is allowed to mix with other colours it will muddy them and spoil the translucency.

The small blots and smudges that often occur when you take a loaded brush over a painting or rest your hand on a still-damp area can also be razored out when dry. If a splash of paint or dirty water falls on the painting, quickly soak up the excess with a twist of tissue or a cotton bud, let it dry and then razor it out gently. If you are intending to apply more paint to the area, rub it down lightly with a soft eraser to smooth the surface, which will have been slightly roughened.

Even professionals, of course, sometimes find that a painting has gone so wrong that small corrections will not suffice or has become so clogged with paint that further work is impossible. If this happens you can, of course, throw it away. But you can also wash out the whole painting, or large parts of it, by putting the paper under running water and sponging the surface. Leave it on its board if you have stretched it. A slight stain may be left, but this can be an advantage as the faint shadow will serve as a drawing for the next attempt. A whole sky or foreground can be removed in this way, while leaving intact those areas with which you are satisfied.

USING GUM WATER.

Gum water, which is gum arabic diluted in water, adds richness to watercolours and keeps the colours bright. It can also be used, as here, as a sort of resist method to create highlights.
1. The tree and hedge are painted in with pure watercolour.
2. A further wash of green is applied, this time mixed with gum water.
3. The area of the central tree is spattered with water, flicked on with a household brush.
4. The central tree is blotted with a rag, so that wherever the water has touched, small areas of paint are lifted off, the gum being soluble in water.
5. The lighter patches of colour give an extra sparkle to the tree, while the addition of the gum water imparts richness to the dark green on either side.

1

2

3

4

5

WATERCOLOUR STEP-BY-STEP

This is an unusually large painting for a watercolour. The head is almost life-size. The colours are gentle and muted with the minimum of tonal contrast. This type of colour scheme, in which there are no dark tones or colours, is known as 'high-key'. Some artists always work in a high key, others always in a low one (using dark or vivid colours with strong contrasts); yet others are happy to work in both, the choice depending on their approach.

This portrait was done from life. The artist made sure that the model was really comfortable before work began, and makes the positions of her hands and feet so that she could resume exactly the same position after breaks. In a painting as subtle as this the drawing had to be very accurate and the tonal contrasts and variations extremely tightly controlled. The artist needed to observe the subject closely without being distracted by movement or complaints about discomfort.

The first stage was to draw a very careful outline, establishing the composition so that each wash could be placed quickly and accurately. The pale colours, as well as the sheer size of the painting, ruled out the possibility of major alterations once the painting had begun. Drawing is particularly important in a portrait, since if the proportions of the features are wrong, or the eyes or mouth placed crookedly, the painting will not only fail as a likeness, but will also lose structural credibility. The drawing need not be elaborate — too many pencil marks can confuse rather than clarify — but it must be clear and accurate enough to provide a guide for the painting; so if you are working from life, make sure that both you and your model have enough time to spare.

1. The photograph shows how different the actual colours were from those the artist has chosen. Even the strongly patterned blanket, which has been given a prominent role in the painting, is much paler and more muted.

2. The drawing was made with a mechanical lead-holder, sometimes called a clutch pencil, into which different leads can be inserted for different purposes. Any unnecessary lines were carefully removed with a soft putty eraser in order not to damage the surface of the paper. Bockingford paper, the one used here, is easily spoiled by excessive erasing.

3. The area around the eyes and brows is one of the most difficult to draw accurately, and the artist pays special attention to the structure and the way the eyes fit into the sockets. Pencil lines can either be rubbed out when the painting is partially done, but quite dry, or left as part of the image.

4. When the pencil drawing was complete the artist began to draw with the brush, painting in the shadow below the top eyelid. The eyes are the focal point of most portraits and need very careful treatment.

5. The next step was to get rid of some of the white paper by applying a pale wash to the background. A No. 2 sable brush was used to work on separate areas right across the painting.

6. The stripes of the blanket were intensified before any further work was done on the face, as this was a very important part of the painting and acted as a key for the colours and tones of the face and hair.

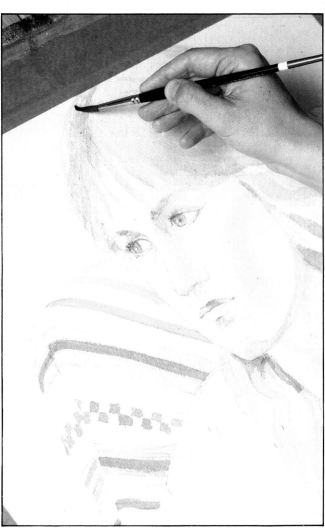

7. Here the artist paints the darkest part of the hair, using a No. 2 sable brush and a mixture of violet, Payne's grey and Indian red. The hair had hitherto been mainly yellow ochre with touches of Indian red.

8. By this stage the paper had been entirely covered, but the painting was somewhat weak and insubstantial, the flesh tones too pale and cool. The artist therefore intensified all the tones, adding warmth to the flesh and giving a more solid feel to the face. The final touches were to paint in the pattern of the blanket and add definition to the hair, so that it formed a pleasing pattern without being fussy.

MATERIALS USED

- ◆ SUPPORT: pre-stretched Bockingford paper, measuring 18 × 16 in/45 × 40 cm.
- ◆ COLOURS: Indian red, yellow ochre, violet, Payne's grey, cobalt blue, ultramarine, alizarin crimson, cadmium red and sap green.
- ◆ BRUSHES AND OTHER EQUIPMENT: Nos. 6 and 2 sable brushes, a mechanical lead-holder and a putty rubber.

8. *Against a Striped Blanket*

◆ CYCLAMEN ◆

Flower arrangements are among the most popular of all still-life subjects. Indeed, they are often regarded as a separate branch of painting. In purely practical terms, however, they are a type of still-life, posing the same problems as well as sharing the major advantage of being a captive subject.

With any group of objects set up as a painting subject the main problem is arrangement, and hence the composition of the painting itself. Flowers in a vase, for example, do not always make a shape that fills a rectangle very well; so it is sometimes necessary to add other elements, such as a plate, some fruit or background drapery. Here the composition is simple but very effective: the table-top, with its checked cloth, provides foreground interest to balance the pattern formed by the flowers themselves against the plain background. It also adds to the impression of solidity and its intersecting diagonal lines provide a pleasing contrast with the curved shapes. Interestingly, the tablecloth was added as an afterthought, when the artist had already painted the flower and pot; without it the character of the painting would have been quite different. When arranging a still-life or flower piece it is helpful to make a few advance sketches, as alterations cannot always be made as easily as they were here.

1. A careful outline drawing was made of the flowers and pot, and then the flowers were painted in with a mixture of cadmium red and purple lake. Particular attention was paid to the arrangement of the spaces created by the flowers against the background.

2. The mid-to-light tones of the leaves in the centre were laid on quite freely, sharper definition being reserved for those at the sides, to form a clear, sharp outline. The colours — emerald green, sap green, Payne's grey and a touch of raw sienna — were put on wet and allowed to mix on the paper.

3. The leaves and flowers were darkened in places and a first wash was then laid on the pot. Here, too, the colours were applied wet and moved around on the paper until the artist was satisfied with the way they had blended together.

4. A very pale wash was put on the underside of the dish, leaving the rim white to stand out against the checks. The blue used was chosen to echo the blue on the pot, and the shadow was added later.

FREEDOM AND LIGHT

5. Here the artist is using the tip of a sable brush to paint the blue checks. Although they were painted carefully, and varied in size and colour to suggest recession, the artist has not attempted to produce perfectly straight or regular lines, which would have looked mechanical and monotonous.

6. The wet-into-wet technique was used for painting the pot, giving it a lively appearance suggestive of light and texture. Widely varying colours were applied with plenty of water and blended into one another. If the paint is too wet, or blends in the wrong way, it can be dabbed off with a sponge or tissue.

MATERIALS USED

◆ SUPPORT: pre-stretched
watercolour paper with a Not
surface, measuring
12 × 16 in/30 × 40 cm.
◆ COLOURS: cadmium red,
alizarin crimson, raw sienna,
purple lake, emerald green,
sap green, lemon yellow,
ultramarine, cobalt blue and
Payne's grey.
◆ BRUSHES: Nos. 7 and 3 sable.

Cyclamen

1

1. This photograph gives an idea of how much paint is needed for a wash over a large area. Until you are used to laying washes it is wise to mix more than you think you will need. This wash, for the sky, is diluted cobalt blue.

◆ DISTANT HILLS ◆

This painting relies for its effect on the use of linear shapes arranged in such a way as to create an atmosphere of gentle harmony. The colour range is very limited, almost monochromatic, and the minimum of detail, even in the foreground, gives the elegantly uncluttered and stylized look characteristic of many Chinese paintings.

One of the artist's main concerns was to indicate the spaciousness and recession of the landscape. He used two methods to do this. The first was aerial perspective, the term used for the way that the features of a landscape become less distinct as they recede, with the colours becoming paler and cooler. Tonal contrasts are greater in the foreground, where the colours are strong and warm. The second method was to allow the tree on the right to go out of the frame at the top, thus clearly indicating that the group of trees is on the picture plane (the front of the painting).

The painting provides an excellent example of the 'classical' approach to watercolour, in which the paint is laid on in a series of thin washes, allowing the brilliance of the white paper to reflect back through them. Unusually, an HP (hot-pressed) paper was used instead of the more popular Not, or cold-pressed, but this artist finds that the smoother paper suits his style, and he mixes a little gum arabic with the water to give extra body and adherence. Each wash, once laid down, has been left without any further paint being laid on top, and the painting was worked from the top downward, with the foreground trees painted over the washes for the sky and hills. It was done in the studio from a sketch and the drawing on the support was restricted to a few lines drawn with an HB pencil.

2

3

2. The wash for the sky, put on with a No.10 squirrel brush, was deliberately laid slightly unevenly to suggest a pale blue sky with a light cloud cover.

3. As soon as the wash for the sky was dry, the same squirrel brush was used to put on a darker shade, with Payne's grey added to the cobalt blue, to the area of the far hills.

4. The second wash had to be darker than that for the sky but not too dark, as the artist knew that he would have to increase the tonal contrasts in the middle distance to suggest its relative nearness to the picture plane.

5 and 6. As each wash has to be allowed to dry before putting on the next, in this particular technique, a hairdrier is sometimes used to hasten the process. The third and fourth washes, darker shades of the second, were laid on next, leaving the whole of the foreground and middle distance still untouched.

7. The tone of the darker area of the middle distance had to be very carefully calculated to make it appear to be in front of the far hills. This wash has been put on slightly thicker in places to suggest the shapes of the trees.

8. The trees in the foreground were worked on next, the darker paint being taken over the background and sky washes. This overlapping device is most successful when the colours are similar; overlapping two quite different colours, for instance red-brown tree trunks over a bright green middle distance, would give a third colour, which could provide a jarring element if not planned.

9 and 10. At this stage both the background and foreground were complete, but the area between the two was still unpainted. Because warm colours tend to advance and cool ones recede, the artist laid a warm greenish wash over this area to make it come forward toward the picture plane.

MATERIALS USED

◆ SUPPORT: pre-stretched watercolour paper with an HP surface, measuring 14 × 21½ in/35 × 53 cm.
◆ COLOURS: cobalt blue, Payne's grey, raw umber and sap green.
◆ BRUSHES: a No. 10 squirrel and a No. 4 sable.
◆ ADDITIONAL EQUIPMENT: a selection of ceramic palettes for mixing the paint; a little gum arabic for mixing with the water.

Distant Hills

TOP, ABOVE AND RIGHT This painting was begun with a monochrome underpainting in dilute cobalt blue, an unusual but deliberate choice of colour, as the blue is repeated throughout the picture. The flowers and drapery were then built up in thicker paint, the method known as 'fat over lean', the background and foliage being left quite thin.

OIL PAINTING TECHNIQUES

ALTHOUGH there are really no hard-and-fast rules in oil painting, it is helpful to have an idea of the various ways in which artists go about things so that you can experiment with different techniques, colour schemes and compositions as you evolve your own particular style. Rules are often useful in a negative way: once you know a rule you can break it for reasons of your own, or 'bend' it, as many artists have done with the rules of perspective. Constable and the French Impressionists broke the rules of their times.

GENERAL PAINTING TECHNIQUES

If you are painting a very simple subject, such as an empty landscape with a wide expanse of sky, there is often no need for an underdrawing or underpainting,

except perhaps a line or two to delineate the horizon. However, for a more complex subject such as a figure study, or perhaps a landscape including people or buildings, a preliminary drawing on the canvas is usually advisable. This enables you to work out the composition and the position of the main elements within it, and to plan the balance of dark colours and light ones. For a portrait or figure painting you will need to establish how you want to place the figure in relation to the background, and you will need to get the proportions of the figure right. If you start an ambitious painting with inadequate drawing you will be forever altering parts of it, which will not only spoil your enjoyment, but will also produce a laboured and overworked painting. Careful planning at the start enables you to be more spontaneous later.

Underdrawings can be done either in pencil or charcoal, the latter being preferable, as it is a broad medium, easier to use freely. To avoid loose charcoal mixing with the paint and muddying it, brush it down lightly with a rag before starting to paint – you will still retain the main lines of the drawing.

Underpainting – another form of drawing but done with a brush – can be made either in monochrome or an understated version of the finished colour scheme, in both cases using paint well thinned with turpentine. If you find a blank canvas somewhat intimidating, you will find that an underpainting overcomes the problem by providing a 'stepping-stone' from which you can build up the succeeding layers of colour with confidence.

A monochrome underpainting should concentrate on the main masses of light and shade, as in the example illustrated, and a coloured one should avoid bright and light colours, as you will want to build up to these as the painting progresses. Nowadays artists often use acrylic paint for underpainting, as this dries much faster than even thinned oil paint, enabling the next stage to proceed immediately.

A good general rule for oil painting – and a very old one – is to work 'fat over lean'. This simply means that in the initial stages the paint should be used fairly thin (diluted with turpentine only) becoming thicker and oilier as the painting progresses. Working in this way reduces the risk of the paint cracking as it dries out. If, however, 'lean' paint is brushed over a layer of 'fat' paint (containing a greater proportion of oil) what happens is that the lean layer dries first, and when the fat layer beneath it eventually starts to dry it contracts, causing the dry layer on top to crack.

Not all paintings, however, are done in stages in this way; many are completed at one sitting, with a minimum of drawing or underpainting or even none at all. This is known as *alla prima* painting, and is much used for landscape or quick portrait studies where the painter wants to record his impressions rapidly in a free and spontaneous manner. The paint is used thickly, with each colour laid down more or less as it will finally appear. When oil paints are used in this way, the colours blend into each other, particularly when one is laid on top of another. This is a feature of *alla prima* painting, known as working 'wet into wet', and was much exploited by the Impressionists, particularly Claude Monet (1840-1926) in his outdoor paintings. For anyone who has not used oils before, *alla prima* is a good way of starting, as it will give you an immediate 'feel' for the medium and force you to work fast without being over-conscious of each brushstroke.

ABOVE This small painting was done by the *alla prima* method, with the paint used quite thickly and put down rapidly with little subsequent alteration.

The photograph (RIGHT) shows colours being blended into one another by working wet into wet. ABOVE a thin layer of transparent red paint is being laid over a dry layer of yellow. This is the technique called glazing, which gives an effect quite unlike that of one layer of thicker paint, as the colour below reflects back through the glaze, giving additional brilliance.

The only drawing for the portrait consisted of a few lines and outlines made with a number 3 bristle brush and thinned paint, **1** after which yellows, blues and warm red-browns were laid on, to be modified and defined later **2**. A rag was used to wipe off some paint from the forehead, cheeks and chin, **3** thus lightening the highlight areas. It was also used to smooth the previously roughly-applied paint in the background, removing some of the excess. **4** and **5** Shadows and highlights were built up in the face and hair,

OIL PAINTING STEP-BY-STEP

THIS portrait was done quite quickly, in only two sessions, and has a fresh and spontaneous quality. Portraits often have to be completed in less time than the painter would perhaps consider ideal, since few sitters have either the time or the inclination to sit in one position for long periods of time. This particular portrait was actually done mainly from the photograph, which was freely adapted to convey the artist's own impression of the subject's colouring and character rather than being used as a 'copy' to be re-produced in paint. He could, of course, have taken much longer over the painting since he was not work-ing from a live model, but he preferred to simulate the conditions of working from life in order to avoid an overworked, tired painting. It is often a good idea to set yourself a time limit in this way, both with portraits and landscapes, and to try to rely on your original impressions of a face or scene.

the paint being blended with a bristle brush and short, dabbing strokes. Because the painting was done on hardboard, which is not very absorbent, only turpentine was used as the medium at this stage, as the addition of oil would have made the paint too sloppy and caused it to dry too slowly.
6 Even so, by the sixth stage the paint had now become too thick and wet to work on satisfactorily, so the whole surface was blotted with newspaper, which removed the excess layer while still leaving a quite distinct image.

1

2

3

4

5

6

RIGHT **7** A piece of newspaper was applied, pressed lightly and lifted off, to remove some of the surplus paint. Blotting paper or towelling can also be used for this purpose.

7

BELOW **8** A rag was used to clean up the area on the face where the paint had become too thick.

8

The painting was begun with an underdrawing in neutral browns and blues, using thinned paint, after which layers of thicker paint were built up. The facial features were left quite undefined in the early stages, emerging only gradually from the broadly treated planes of the face, and the scarf was added later almost as an afterthought. All areas of the painting were worked on at the same time, the whole canvas being covered almost immediately, so that the relationship of the tones and colours could be assessed, balanced and altered where necessary. When the head was reasonably complete the artist decided to lighten the colours of the background, which also gave him an opportunity to correct and redefine the outline of the face. The tones and colours of the flesh were then adjusted in relation to the new background, and the relatively bright colours of the scarf blocked in to balance them. In oil painting, almost any such alterations can be made, but it is easier to work light over dark because white is the most opaque colour. If the painting had started with a light background, an attempt to change it to a dark one would probably have been unsatisfactory.

Because the painting was done quickly, there was no time to allow the paint to dry between stages, so a rag or a piece of newspaper was used from time to time to lightly blot the surface, removing the excess paint. A rag was also used to spread the paint in the background areas and to lighten the highlights in the early stages. Such techniques are particularly useful when working on a non-absorbent surface such as hardboard, which can easily become so overloaded with paint that successive layers stir it up and muddy it.

ABOVE **9** and RIGHT **10** Using a small brush, the artist begins to work on the more detailed areas of the painting to define the hitherto vague facial features.

MATERIALS USED

- Support: primed hardboard 45 × 30 cm (18 × 12 in)
- Brushes: number 3 flat bristle and a number 5 round sable for the fine details
- Colours: titanium white, ivory black, cadmium yellow, yellow ochre, vandyke brown, cobalt blue, ultramarine, chrome oxide and vermilion, and the painting mediums were turpentine and linseed oil

10

11

12

ABOVE **11** and **12** When the painting was almost finished it became clear to the artist that it needed to be lightened in tone; so he overpainted the background, taking the opportunity to correct the outline of the face at the same time, and then adjusted the colours and tones of the flesh, blending the paint with light brushstrokes. He then altered the righthand side of the background again, so that from being the darker side it became the lighter one – almost white. The scarf, seen in the finished painting, was not originally planned as part of the composition, but the heightened tones and colours seemed to need a balance, and it was added as a final touch. This portrait provides an excellent example of the way in which oil paintings can be altered again and again without loss of quality.

OPPOSITE Earlier stages involved covering the face with a reddish glaze, giving a warmth and glow to the flesh. The effect of this is clearly visible in both the detail of the brow area and in the finished painting.

TEA-CADDY ON A WINDOW SILL

THIS small, quietly harmonious painting, with its limited range of colours and simple subject, provides a contrast with the one on page 44, where the approach is quite different. It also illustrates the way in which colour and composition can be used quite deliberately to create mood: here there are no jarring compositional elements and no bright or discordant colours, but the effect is far from dull – just pleasantly peaceful.

Most people have one or two items about their homes that seem to suggest an idea for a painting, and in this case the artist was attracted to the swelling curves of the pot and its decorative motif. In order to highlight these qualities, he chose to make the composition a geometric one, in which the horizontals and verticals of the window frame and shutter act as a foil for the curved and rounded shapes. The composition is very carefully balanced, with the strip of blue-grey in the foreground just slightly narrower than the window sill above, and the rectangle on the right large enough to be 'read' as the view through the window but not so large as to dominate the painting. The verticals of the window frame have been carefully planned so that they do not interfere with the dominant shapes of the pot and bowl, and the slanting shadows on the left, which appear in the photograph as very distinct areas of tone, are merely hinted at by a very slightly darker colour at the top left.

The paint has been applied very carefully and meticulously, with sable brushes used to build up thin layers, and the support, a fine-grained canvas, was chosen as particularly suitable for this kind of painting. For a picture like this it is important that the straight lines should really be straight – an accidentally slanting vertical line, for example, would provide just the jarring element the artist has been at pains to avoid – so masking tape was used to aid the process. At one time such techniques were considered rather 'mechanical', and frowned upon, but it is extremely difficult to draw a straight line freehand, let alone paint one with a brush, and there is no reason why masking tape or rulers should not be used.

The range of colours used was deliberately very small – just two blues, a green, grey, black and yellow. It can be a useful discipline to limit your colours in this way, choosing just one or two colours and their complementaries (blue and yellow, as here, or red and green) plus greys and browns. It may cut down your choices, but this can also be an advantage as you will have fewer to make, and you may find that your painting achieves a harmony and unity that it might not have had with a whole range of colours at your disposal. It will also teach you far more about mixing colours than reading a whole book on the subject.

1

2

TOP **1** AND ABOVE **2** As the composition is so simple, no underdrawing was necessary. Instead, the main elements were quickly blocked in, using thin paint and a sable brush, in more or less the colours that appear in the finished painting.

3

LEFT **3** At this stage a bristle brush was used, as the paint was rather thicker (though still relatively thin). The blue of the pot was built up using a mixture of ultramarine and white, with white and Payne's grey used for the window sill. Payne's grey is a useful and versatile colour, with a slight mauvish tinge. Here it appears quite warm in relation to the deep blue. A mixture of black and white would have given a much less 'alive' quality.

LEFT **4** Masking tape was applied to the line which separates the edge of the window frame from the little rectangle of landscape beyond. This allowed the paint to be applied quite freely on the window-frame area.

BELOW LEFT **5** The tape was then lifted off, leaving a clean, straight edge. To use this method successfully the paint must be quite thin and at least semi-dry; otherwise the tape, when lifted off, will take the top layer of paint with it.

4

5

RIGHT **6** AND BELOW RIGHT **7**
At this stage, several thin layers of paint had been built up one over the other, but the details, which give a crisp definition to the finished painting, had not been added. In the detail (RIGHT) a small sable brush is being used to paint the fine lines and small cracks at the bottom of the shutter. If you look at the finished painting you will see that this delicate diagonal line is actually vital to the composition, leading the eye to the pot and bowl, which are the focal points.

OPPOSITE The brickwork was painted in a mixture of Payne's grey, yellow ochre and white, with viridian and white used for the mini-landscape through the window. Great care must be taken with an area such as this; if the tonal contrast were too great or the colours too bright the landscape would 'jump' forward, assuming too much visual importance and conflicting with the foreground. Viridian, being a cool, rather blue green, is useful for receding backgrounds.

MATERIALS USED

- Support: small, ready-primed, fine-grained canvas only 30.5 × 25.4 cm (12 × 10 in)
- Brushes: small sable and a number 8 round bristle
- Colours: titanium white, ivory black, Payne's grey, yellow ochre, cadmium yellow pale, viridian, ultramarine and Prussian blue

6

7

STILL-LIFE WITH WATERMELON

THIS still-life, while very different from the one shown on page 35 in its use of thick paint and bright colours, has a rather similar atmosphere of simple, quiet harmony. One of the most difficult aspects of still-life painting is deciding on the initial arrangement; it is only too easy to buy up a greengrocer's entire stock and then find yourself unable to arrive at a satisfactory way of arranging the different elements, or to rush around the house collecting bowls, plates and vases which, when placed together, don't seem to add up to anything you want to paint. Here, as can be seen in the photograph, the artist has chosen a simple arrangement, but one in which the shapes are balanced very carefully.

The composition of the painting is based on a triangle with the point at the top left, and the circular shapes of the plate and half melon intersecting at different angles. The smaller piece of melon echoes the triangle, while the strawberries in the foreground both break up the area of white space and give a feeling of solidity by establishing the plane on which they rest. If you mask them out with your finger you can see how drastically the composition would be weakened and how the main elements would then appear to float in space. The artist has chosen to ignore the line created by the back edge of the table, treating the table top and background as a flat area of 'negative space'; treating the table and wall as separate planes would have detracted from the composition and reduced the importance of the main shapes, which appear almost as though 'carved out' of the space.

A variety of painting techniques has been used to create an interesting paint surface, the first step being a coloured underpainting in very washy paint, after which areas were built up and defined in much thicker paint. The watermelon was given texture by spattering paint on to the surface from a stiff-haired brush; a pencil was used to draw into the fruit; and the white background is very slightly textured with just-visible brushstrokes.

RIGHT 1 A faint underdrawing was done with pencil to position the main elements of the composition, which were then blocked in with heavily-diluted paint.

2

3

TOP RIGHT **2** AND ABOVE **3** As soon as the underpainting was dry the artist began to define the separate pieces of fruit, building up the highlights in thick, juicy paint.

1

The artist then drew into the dry paint with a pencil, OPPOSITE **4** a technique which has a dual function in this case as it gives texture and visual interest to the fruit as well as taking down the tones without the necessity for overpainting.

LEFT **5** Until now the strawberries had been left as just bold brushstrokes of dark red, but here the artist has given them shape and form, painting the highlights in a light pink and the leaves and stems in bright green.

BELOW **6** The final touch was to modify the shapes by working back into them with white paint and to paint the shadows in blue-grey, clearly outlined on the white background and establishing the plane of the table top.

5

6

RIGHT **7** The watermelon required special treatment, as the texture is an important element of the painting. The artist has chosen a technique he frequently uses – spattering paint from a stiff-haired brush (a toothbrush is often used for this purpose). In order not to splash paint on the rest of the painting he has cut a mask from newspaper, leaving exposed only those areas to be textured. Two tones were used for the spattering, one lighter and one darker than the mid-tone of the underpainting, the paler one echoing the highlights on the strawberries.

BELOW RIGHT **8** The tones and colours were chosen with great care as they had to be light or dark enough to show up, but not so sharply contrasting as to 'jump' off the surface.

7

OPPOSITE In the finished painting the pencil drawing is still just visible on the banana and the apple, and the same technique has been used on the smaller piece of watermelon and on small areas of the shadow under it and the plate. It is touches such as these that give a painting that special 'something', creating extra interest and liveliness; but they should never be allowed to become too important – special techniques are tools, not ends in themselves.

MATERIALS USED

- Support: bought, ready-primed canvas board 51 × 40 cm (20 × 16 in)
- Brushes: number 12 white bristle and a number 4 hog's hair, with a 2.5-cm (1-in) housepainting brush used for the spattering
- Colours: titanium white, yellow ochre, vermilion, cadmium red, cadmium yellow, sap green, cobalt blue and Payne's grey, a range consisting almost entirely of good, strong primaries

8

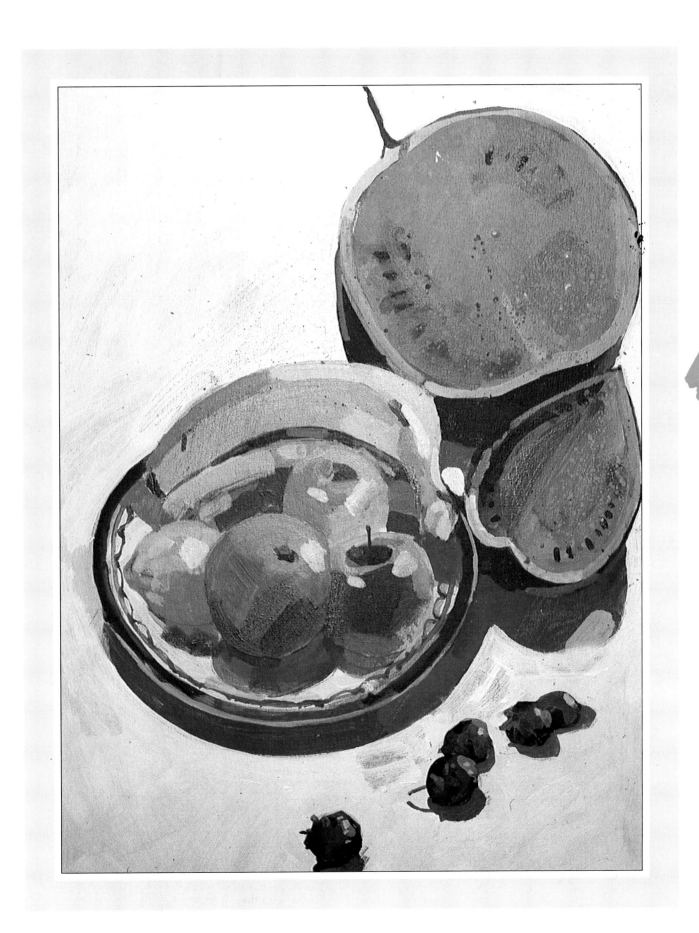

FLOWERS ON A WINDOW SILL

ALTHOUGH you would not think it from looking at the painting, this is actually a very difficult subject, presenting a good many problems. The main one is how to deal with the picture planes – the foreground and the space beyond it – in such a way as to create a feeling of space and recession while still retaining the unity of composition which is the hallmark of a successful painting. If the background is allowed to recede too much it will run the risk of becoming dull, but if it comes forward too much it will overwhelm the foreground. The foreground itself has to be given much thought too; otherwise the vase of flowers, which is the focal point, could assume too little importance, and not be strong enough to balance the landscape beyond. Here the artist has solved all the problems very cleverly; the foreground has been given extra importance and interest by the inclusion of the window blind and curtain on one side and the top of a chair on the other, so that an interesting composition exists even without the buildings in the background. The hill village and mountains beyond have been allowed to recede just a little so that they read as a separate and more distant picture plane, but they are still very definitely part of the painting, a landscape in themselves, neatly framed by the verticals of the window. The artist has been lucky, as the hilly terrain has provided a landscape that fits the window; a flatter view would have necessitated a quite different treatment in terms of composition.

The colours used for the landscape echo the deep blues of the vase and cushion, but are slightly nearer one another in tone so that they do not come forward and fight with the foreground. As he worked, the artist had frequently to half-close his eyes, which makes it easier to assess tonal contrasts, and to make small adjustments. Although the colours are vivid and the tonal contrasts bold, the paint itself has been used fairly thinly, in a technique akin to that of watercolour, with small areas of unpainted white canvas left showing in the finished picture. This has given the painting a fresh, sparkling appearance, unlike that achieved by areas of applied white (though there are such areas too). This lively, spontaneous effect is enhanced by the quite rough and sketchy treatment of the window frame and sill.

1

2

TOP **1** This is a complex subject, in which the correct placing of the verticals and horizontals is just as important as the bowl of flowers and the chair top; so a preliminary pencil drawing was made on the canvas to position all the elements in relation to each other. The main shapes were then blocked in in thin colour, the window frame being laid down first, with the bowl and chair painted over the resulting grid. This simple device of overlapping also serves to create depth. At this stage the background has been left as an undefined area of grey-blue in a mid-tone which will act as a key for the more specific tones and colours to be added later. The dark greens of the leaves (ABOVE) **2** provide the key for the darker tones of the foreground.

LEFT **3** Once the tones of the foreground were established, the artist began to work on the buildings in the landscape, carefully relating the shapes and colours to those in the foreground.

Here yellow ochre is being applied thinly to the roofs, and the row of cypress trees has already been painted, echoing and balancing the leaves on the flowers.

3

4

5

ABOVE **4** AND RIGHT **5** Now the artist works on the flowers, deepening the greens, heightening the reds and yellows, and at the same time deepening the blue of

the vase. Small areas of the white canvas have been left unpainted, giving a sparkling effect to the leaves and flowers.

RIGHT **6** This detail of the flowers and leaves against the background buildings shows the way the greater tonal contrasts make the flowers stand out just enough to be read as being on a nearer plane. White paint has been applied to the tops of the flowers where they catch the light.

OPPOSITE The artist worked over all the areas of the painting at the same time, moving from foreground to background and constantly making small adjustments. The final touches were the fine lines of white to indicate the fold of the curtain on the left, and the addition of a cushion to the chair. This forms a triangle just intersecting the horizontal of the window sill.

MATERIALS USED

- Support: bought canvas board 51 × 40 cm (20 × 16 in)
- Brushes: bristle, number 12 flat and number 6 filbert. Turpentine was used to dilute the paint in the early stages
- Colours: titanium white, vermilion, cadmium red, cobalt violet, raw umber, Indian red, yellow ochre, chrome green, oxide of chromium, ultramarine blue and cerulean blue. (Vermilion is a very expensive colour, but is occasionally necessary for a subject like this, which relies on vivid and pure colours)

6